save the . . .
PENGUINS

by **Anita Sanchez**
with an introduction
by **Chelsea Clinton**

PHILOMEL

This is another story for Laine.

PHILOMEL
An imprint of Penguin Random House LLC
1745 Broadway, New York, New York 10019

First published in the United States of America by Philomel,
an imprint of Penguin Random House LLC, 2024

Text copyright © 2024 by Chelsea Clinton

Photo credits: page 2: © Goinyk/Adobe Stock; page 4: © Paul/Adobe Stock; page 7:
© Brian Lambert/Adobe Stock; page 10: © RLS Photo/Adobe Stock; page 15: Goinyk/
Adobe Stock; page 18: © Tarpan/Adobe Stock; page 20: © Danita Delimont/Adobe Stock;
page 24: © MaryCatalan/Adobe Stock; page 27: © Danita Delimont/Adobe Stock; page 33:
© Silvia Pascual/Adobe Stock; page 37: © Vasilii/Adobe Stock; page 43: © Jan Will/Adobe
Stock; page 48: © willtu/Adobe Stock; page 50: © Anita Sanchez/Penguins International;
page 54: © Julija/Adobe Stock; page 58: © Song_about_summer/Adobe Stock; page 64:
© Simon Ebel/Adobe Stock; page 68: © ondrejprosicky/Adobe Stock

Philomel is a registered trademark of Penguin Random House LLC.
The Penguin colophon is a registered trademark of Penguin Books Limited.

Visit us online at PenguinRandomHouse.com.

Library of Congress Cataloging-in-Publication Data is available.

ISBN 9780593624494 (hardcover)
ISBN 9780593624500 (paperback)

1st Printing

Printed in the United States of America

LSCC

Edited by Talia Benamy and Jill Santopolo • Design by Lily Qian
Text set in Calisto MT Pro

save the . . .

Dear Reader,

When I was around your age, my favorite animals were dinosaurs and elephants. I wanted to know everything I could about triceratopses, stegosauruses and other dinosaurs that had roamed our earth millions of years ago. Elephants, though, captured my curiosity and my heart. The more I learned about the largest animals on land today, the more I wanted to do to help keep them and other endangered species safe forever.

So I joined organizations working around the world to support endangered species and went to our local zoo to learn more about conservation efforts close to home (thanks to my parents and grandparents). I tried to learn as much as I could about how we can ensure animals and plants don't go extinct like the dinosaurs, especially since it's the choices that we're making that pose the greatest threat to their lives today.

The choices we make don't have to be huge to make

a real difference. When I was in elementary school, I used to cut up the plastic rings around six-packs of soda, glue them to brightly colored construction paper (purple was my favorite) and hand them out to whomever would take one in a one-girl campaign to raise awareness about the dangers that plastic six-pack rings posed to marine wildlife around the world. I learned about that from a book—*50 Simple Things Kids Can Do to Save the Earth*—which helped me understand that you're never too young to make a difference and that we all can change the world. I hope that this book will inform and inspire you to help save this and other endangered species. There are tens of thousands of species that are currently under threat, with more added every year. We have the power to save those species, and with your help, we can.

Sincerely,

Chelsea Clinton

save the . . .
PENGUINS

CONTENTS

1

THE PARTY BIRDS

When you meet a penguin, the first thing you notice is that he's all dressed up for a party! At least it looks that way. A penguin's crisp black-and-white coloring looks like a fancy tuxedo—all that's missing is a bow tie.

The first European explorers who encountered penguins centuries ago weren't exactly sure what the strange creatures were: Birds, mammals, or maybe a kind of fish? At first glance, it seemed these animals waddling along

All dressed up for a party!

the ice couldn't be birds. Penguins can't fly like most birds can. On land, they walk around with tiny steps, waving seemingly useless wings. They can go faster when they lie down and slide on their bellies over the smooth ice. But afoot, these plump, clumsy birds are, well . . . kind of like fish out of water.

But once penguins dive into the ocean, everything changes. Their black-and-white forms zoom through the water like spaceships at warp speed. Their strong wings act as powerful oars in the water. They use their large, webbed feet to steer, weaving and darting this way and that. Penguins are the fastest-swimming birds on the planet. Some types of penguins can swim twenty miles an hour—about twice as fast as most people can run! And some penguins can dive deep into the freezing depths of the sea, as far down as eighteen hundred feet deep. That's the length of a hundred-story building. Penguins can also leap out of the water and splash back in again, playing in the waves like dolphins.

But of course, no matter how good they are in the water, penguins aren't fish—they're birds. If you run your hand over a penguin's glossy head, you'll find they have something no

Penguins jet through the water with amazing speed.

fish has ever had: feathers. Penguins are flight-less birds, but they still need feathers.

The short, thick feathers overlap each other like tiles on a roof, making the penguin's body streamlined and fast in the water. The thick coat of feathers also keeps the birds' body warmth close to the skin and helps to keep the cold out. Penguins have more feathers per square inch than any other bird—some have a hundred feathers per square inch. These feathers are perfect for long, cold swims, since penguins usually spend more time in the water than they do on land.

Which Penguin Is Which?

Penguins all wear tuxedos, but they aren't all alike! There are more than one kind of penguin. In fact, there are eighteen different species of these adorable birds.

You've probably seen pictures of penguins on Antarctic ice and snow. But not all penguins live where it's cold. Only four species of penguins live in Antarctica, which is the icy continent that surrounds the South Pole. Some species of penguins live on sunny, sandy beaches! Others live on the rocky coastlines of Australia and New Zealand, on the southernmost tip of Africa, or along the edge of South America. One species lives farther north, hanging out on the remote Galapagos Islands, which are right on the equator (the imaginary line around the middle of the earth).

Penguins come in many shapes and sizes. There are Rockhopper penguins and Yellow-eyed penguins—guess how they got their names. There are Chinstrap penguins that look like they're wearing a little black cap with a strap tied under their chin. The biggest penguin is the Emperor, which is about four feet tall— probably about as tall as you are. The smallest is the doll-sized Fairy penguin, which would only come up about as high as your knee and weighs about two pounds.

But one thing almost all penguins have in common: they appear to be wearing a dark

Penguins come in all shapes and sizes—and hairdos!

jacket and white shirtfront (most penguins are black and white, but some, like the Fairy penguin, are bluish gray). Yet a penguin's color scheme isn't for looking good at a party—it helps the birds survive.

On a sunny day, if you put your hand on a dark surface and then on a light one, the dark one will feel warmer. This is because dark colors absorb more of the sun's energy. On cold days, penguins turn their dark backs to the sun and soak up that nice warmth.

But for a penguin species like the Humboldt penguins that live in South America, the temperature might get up into the seventies (Fahrenheit) or even higher. In penguin habitats near the sea, there are very few trees to give shade. In their warm suits of feathers, the penguins could get dangerously overheated. So if they feel too warm, they turn to face the sun. Their white tummies reflect the heat, helping them keep their cool.

Another great thing about a penguin's fancy feathers is that they provide a type of camouflage called countershading. This is especially useful because penguins spend so much time in the water. In the cold ocean, there are lots of hungry jaws hunting for food. Sharks, killer whales, and seals all prey on penguins. To anything looking up, a swimming bird's light stomach blends with the sunlit water on the surface. To anything looking down, the darker back blends with the darkness of the deep water. This helps penguins to hide from predators that might want to have them for lunch. It also helps them sneak up on their own prey: fish and other sea animals they need for food.

A Wet Restaurant

The ocean is where all penguins go when it's time for dinner. The hungry birds dive headfirst into the water and swim in search of food. They can see really well underwater, and while hunting they keep a sharp eye out for a school of fish or a tasty jellyfish swimming by.

Fast-swimming penguins swoop down on their meal with open mouths. Almost anything small enough for a penguin to swallow might be on the menu: squid, crabs, little shrimps called krill, and fish, such as sardines and anchovies. The bird grabs its prey with its sharp beak and often swallows it whole.

You might be able to hold your breath underwater for a whole minute, or maybe a little more. But a penguin can stay underwater for a

Krill: a tasty treat for a penguin.

lot longer. Penguin dives usually last six minutes or so, but on its deepest dives, an Emperor penguin can hold its breath for almost half an hour.

In the cold areas where most penguins swim, a person couldn't stay in the water for more than a few minutes. But penguins can swoop through the water for hours without freezing. That's because they're wearing a sort of oily overcoat. At the base of a penguin's tail there's a gland that oozes out an oily slime. The penguin uses its beak to smear the oil over its feathers before it jumps in the water. The oil keeps its feathery coat nice and dry, which keeps the penguin cozy and warm. Even in Antarctic waters, penguins can spend hours swimming among the icebergs. After a long dive, the penguin surfaces to get some air, bobbing on the water like a duck, then glides underwater to hunt again.

Back to Shore

Penguins do get out of the water every now and then. When mating season rolls around, they need to find a safe place to lay eggs and raise their young. They time their nesting so the chicks will hatch just as there's the largest amount of fish, krill, and other seafood available to feed the hungry babies.

For any bird, nesting season is a time of challenges. Penguins have to solve some especially hard problems, including how to raise their babies in a habitat that's cold, damp, and almost treeless. Each species of penguin has a different place it calls home and a different way of nesting. But one thing all penguins know: it takes two partners working together to raise a baby penguin.

2

IT TAKES TWO

Penguins may be super fast in the water, but they're slowpokes on land. They're almost helpless against predators, such as seabirds and seals, that might want to steal their eggs or eat their babies. Penguins can't outrun predators that might attack them, and since they don't have teeth or powerful claws, they can't fight back. But there's safety in numbers. When it's time to raise the kids, most kinds of penguins head to a nesting area called a rookery.

The same rookeries are usually used for many years, as penguins faithfully return to them every time. Some rookeries have thousands or even millions of birds.

With so many other penguins around, it's a good place for a young male penguin to meet a female. He shows off, strutting around with wings stretched out and singing his heart out. If his loud *yawp yawp* gets the attention of a female, she strolls over to check him out. The two birds might bow to each other or slap each other on the back with their wings. They call back and forth, getting to know each other's voices. If they decide to stick together, they will likely be partners for many years.

After the birds mate, it's time for the female to lay her eggs—but where? Most birds build nests in trees, but where penguins live, there

A pair of penguins ready to work together.

are hardly any trees to be seen. And penguins couldn't fly up into branches or climb trees anyway. The only place for penguins to nest is down low.

Where to Build a Nest?

The place to put a nest depends on the kind of habitat a penguin lives in. The beach-loving Yellow-eyed penguin digs a burrow in the sand. Galapagos penguins nest in small caves and clefts in the rocks. African penguins, which live at the tip of South Africa, nest on sandy flats where there are sparse bushes and shrubs. They might build a nest hidden under a bush.

Humboldt penguins have lived on islands with other birds for many centuries. The birds' poop, called guano, has piled up many feet thick there over time. The soil on the islands is too hard and stony for penguins to dig into, so they burrow into the soft guano layers to make a little cavelike den for nesting.

What a penguin uses for nest building also depends on what materials it can find nearby. Adélie penguins, which live on rocky shores, build a nest of rocks piled neatly in a circle. They're very fussy about which rocks they use and sometimes get into quarrels with one another over the perfect rock. Once in a while they even steal rocks from each other's nests. The more polite Gentoo penguins, which nest on cold, rocky beaches, use pebbles, sticks, and even feathers other birds have dropped. One such nest was made of seventeen hundred pebbles and seventy tail feathers.

Once the nest or burrow is ready, the female penguin lays her eggs. Penguins have small families—they generally incubate only two eggs a year. The partners take turns guarding the eggs and sitting on them to keep them warm. While one penguin is on incubation duty, the other will jump in the water to hunt for food and could be gone for many days. They take turns back and forth for several weeks until the eggs are ready to hatch.

Finding the perfect place to hatch their eggs and raise their young is a tough problem for any

Hi, Mom!

bird—they have to figure out how to avoid predators, get enough food, and teach their babies how to survive. Each bird does this in a slightly different way. But there's one species of penguin that really, really, really does it the hard way.

It's Cold Out There!

Think back to the last time you had a snow day. No school! Time for you to go outside and throw snowballs and build a snowman. But when you got cold, you could always come indoors and warm up. Imagine living outdoors for months at a time, sleeping on a snowbank, huddling outside during a blizzard. That's what Emperor penguins do.

Emperors are one of the few penguin species that spend their entire lives in the Antarctic. Unlike most other penguins, which nest in the springtime, Emperors do it in the winter. And winters in Antarctica are the coldest ones in the world. The temperature might drop to 80° below zero Fahrenheit, with bitterly cold winds sweeping across the snow and ice. But even in these freezing conditions, every fall Emperor penguins return to the same breeding ground on the Antarctic ice that their parents used, and their parents before them.

It would be too cold even for penguins to nest on the flat, windswept layers of ice that cover the sea in an Antarctic wintertime. So the Emperor penguins head away from the ocean, moving inland to their rookery, which is usually located near cliffs and mounds of ice that will protect them from the worst of the winds.

But Emperors don't build any kind of nest.

Penguins like to hang out together.

Standing on the ice, the female lays a single round egg. Right away, her partner nudges the egg onto his own large, flat feet. A fold of skin on his tummy hangs over the egg and covers it snugly. Under this loose fold there's a patch of skin called a brood patch that doesn't have any feathers so the penguin's body heat can keep the egg nice and warm. The father penguin gets the precious egg safely settled on his feet. And then, he waits.

He has to wait for his partner to get back from work. As soon as the egg is laid, the mother penguin hurries off to her job, which is getting food for their baby chick that is soon to hatch. She leaves before the egg hatches, and it's a long commute—she has to go all the way back to open water to hunt for food. But as the winter gets colder, the sea freezes farther and farther out. Her hunting place in the ocean might be fifty miles away from the rookery, depending on how far out from land the seawater has frozen. And penguins don't walk very fast.

Meanwhile, Dad keeps on waiting. He's not alone, because around him are all the other fathers balancing their eggs on their feet. When the freezing Antarctic winds blow, they snuggle together in a tight group, much like a football huddle. The penguins on the outside of the group shove their way inside as the ones in the center move out. In the tight huddle of penguin bodies, it can get so warm that the penguins in the center actually begin to get too hot. They sometimes have to push their way out of the huddle and eat some snow to cool themselves down.

Days pass, then weeks. All this time, the female penguin is busily diving and hunting for food. She eats as much krill, fish, and other goodies as she can, fattening herself up. Then she eats even more, beakful after beakful of food, but she doesn't digest it fully. Instead, she holds the food in her crop, a pouch inside her throat. When her crop is packed full, she starts the long waddle back to her family.

More weeks pass, then months. The mother's journey can take up to three months or even more, and this whole time, the father penguin has had no food. Dad is getting thinner and thinner. There's not a thing to eat on the snowy plain, but all he can do is wait.

Finally, the baby penguin inside the shell has grown big enough to hatch. The egg cracks open, and out comes the baby, looking like

Dad is patiently keeping the egg safe and warm.

a fluffy gray ball. The baby doesn't yet have the thick feathers that will keep it warm and would freeze in just a few minutes out on the ice. So Dad cuddles the youngster in his brood pouch and waits some more.

Finally, a dark speck appears on the horizon. It's Mom!

Upon arriving, she coughs up the partly digested food in her crop. The baby feeds hungrily. Then Mom carefully takes the baby onto her own feet and cuddles it next to her own brood patch. Now Dad can head off to get a meal.

Mom keeps the baby warm for many more weeks, until the baby has grown enough feathers to keep it from freezing. The long winter has almost passed, and spring is coming—the bitter weather is finally warming up. Now they can head to the sea so the parents can teach the baby how to hunt.

Chicks start out looking like they're dressed up in fuzzy gray pajamas. Though they quickly grow the usual black-and-white penguin markings on their heads, for many weeks their bodies keep the thick fluffy feathers they had when they first hatched. These feathers help keep them warm but aren't yet the slick, waterproof feather coat that their parents have. So the chicks have to wait at the water's edge for the adults to come back from the hunt and feed them. It takes about three months for the chicks to be ready for their first dip in the sea.

Penguins on the Red Carpet

Most penguins live in faraway, remote places that are hard for people to reach, except by sea. Unless we visit penguins in a zoo, few of us are ever likely to meet a penguin in real life. But penguins are some of the most popular animals on Earth, and one reason is that they make great movie stars!

In 2005 a French filmmaker named Luc Jacquet made a movie about Emperor penguins and their struggle to raise their babies. It is called *March of the Penguins*. Many people thought that a two-hour documentary about penguins standing around in the cold wouldn't be a big success. There weren't even any humans in the movie! But *March of the Penguins* was a surprise smash hit. Audiences flocked to theaters to cheer on the penguins on their

It's hard not to fall in love with a baby penguin.

long trek. They laughed at the penguins tobog-ganing along on their stomachs and rooted for the tiny fluffy chicks balanced on their fathers' feet. The movie won an Oscar and made more than seventy million dollars.

Then a cartoon movie called *Happy Feet* came along. This musical about a lovable, tap-dancing penguin turned even more people into penguin fans. All over the world, people have fallen in love with these funny little birds. But while penguins were becoming more and more popular, their cold, watery world was changing fast. Both on the land and in the sea, penguins have been coming up against some scary problems they have never faced before.

3

PENGUINS IN TROUBLE

As we've seen, penguins are speedy in the water but super slow on land. Adult penguins can only walk about two miles per hour at top speed. And because they don't have a lot of predators on land, they aren't as wary of human beings as most wild animals are. People who have traveled where penguins live say that these birds are likely to walk right up to a person, waving their flippers, apparently glad to meet them. Many people report curious penguins surrounding visitors, gently tugging at shoelaces with their beaks.

As soon as the first European sailors encountered penguins in the fifteenth century, they began hunting the friendly birds. It's all too easy to hunt animals that don't run away. Penguins were used as a source of food for hungry sailors craving fresh meat. The birds' skins and the oil from their bodies were also valuable. Penguin eggs were often gathered and eaten, in spite of the fact that penguin eggs taste like a penguin's favorite food—fish.

But during the last century people began to realize that penguins were in trouble. In 1959 many nations, including the United States, signed an agreement called the Antarctic Treaty, which protected all species of penguins from hunting and egg-gathering humans. That was a huge step in the right direction, but it's not enough. Penguins are still being harmed when people also take or destroy the resources the birds need to survive. To help prevent that, we need to focus on protecting the places where penguins live. That means learning more about the penguins' lifestyle, including where they go, what they eat, and where they breed.

An organization of scientists called the International Union for Conservation of Nature (IUCN) keeps track of endangered species of plants, animals, and fungi on a list called the IUCN Red List of Threatened Species™. The threatened animals are put into seven categories. Least Concern and Near Threatened mean the animals are mostly doing okay, but scientists are a little worried about them. Vulnerable means that it's likely that soon the animal will become endangered. Endangered and Critically Endangered mean that there is a strong risk that the animal may become extinct. Extinct in the Wild means the animal doesn't exist in nature anymore—they can only be found in zoos or research centers. The last category is Extinct— and that, of course, means the species is gone forever. The IUCN keeps track of penguins as part of its work, and that work is different for each type of penguin.

Penguins Don't All Have the Same Problems

Remember, there are many species of penguins. Some of them are doing better than others. A few penguin species, such as the Gentoo penguin, are found on the IUCN Red List under the category of Least Concern.

Their populations have stayed more or less the same in recent years. Gentoo penguins number about six hundred thousand today. Adélie penguin populations are even increasing slightly. But more than half of the world's penguin species are in serious trouble.

Humboldt penguins are just one of the species facing serious problems.

Some species of penguins, such as the Humboldt, are listed as Vulnerable. Humboldt populations are getting smaller because they are losing their habitat. The deep layers of guano they depend on for their nesting sites may seem icky, but surprisingly, guano is a highly valuable resource that people want. Because bird poop contains so many nutrients, it makes really good fertilizer for growing plants. People mine the guano, digging it up and loading it onto ships to sell to farmers who use it to fertilize their crops. But removing the guano makes it harder and harder for Humboldt penguins to find safe places to nest. On their rocky, barren islands, there's no other place to keep penguin chicks protected during nesting season. The baby penguins can't survive without shelter, not only from cold and rain but also from overheating on sunny days. There were once hundreds of thousands of Humboldt penguins, but there are now only about twenty-four thousand left in the world, mostly living along the coasts of Chile and Peru.

Five species of penguins are listed as Endangered. These species are at risk partly because they are found in only a very few places. The Erect-crested penguin breeds only on two small clusters of islands off the coast of New Zealand, and nowhere else in the world. If anything bad, such as a disease or a storm, harmed some of these rare species, there may not be enough of them left to recover. Galapagos penguins, Northern Rockhopper penguins, African penguins, and Yellow-eyed penguins have the same problem—they're found only in a few tiny areas. The Yellow-eyed penguin is one of the rarest penguin species in the world. There were more than seven thousand of them only twenty years ago. Now only about three thousand adults remain.

But why are so many penguin populations

shrinking? Penguins have a lot of tough problems to deal with, and all of them are caused by people.

Plastic: The Problem That Won't Go Away

One huge predicament for penguins comes from something that we use every day: plastic.

Plastic takes a long time to break down and decompose. If you drop a paper cup or a paper bag into the water, it will decompose quickly, within a few days. But plastic litter takes much longer, sometimes many years, to breaks down (and even then, it never breaks down entirely), which means that little pieces of plastic trash stick around for a really long time. Every plastic bag, plastic straw, or plastic bottle that gets dropped on the ground can wash into a stream

This is where plastic litter ends up.

or river that leads to the ocean. It's horrifying to think of how much plastic ends up in our oceans—more than seven million tons of it, every year.

A big part of the issue is that most plastic floats. This type of litter doesn't just sink to the bottom of the sea and vanish. It hangs around, in easy reach of passing fish, whales, seabirds, sea turtles, seals—and penguins. To a hungry penguin, a plastic bag looks like a tasty jellyfish. Brightly colored plastic bottle caps or straws also catch the eye of hunting penguins, which have good vision underwater.

And even worse than the plastic they can see is the plastic they can't see. Microplastics are bits of plastic less than five millimeters long, which is about the size of the point of a pencil. The tiny bits of microplastic float around and get eaten by small fish and other animals without them even realizing it. So penguins may eat plastic themselves, or eat fish that have eaten plastic. Either way, it ends up in their stomachs. Sometimes the plastic gets stuck, clogging their digestive systems so they can't absorb food. And plastics, which are made from oil, also give off toxic chemicals that can make penguins sick and weak.

Deadly Oil

Another thing we use every day is a big threat to penguins: petroleum oil.

People use oil for fuel to run our cars, heat our houses, and create electricity to power everything from lamps to computers to cell phones. It is shipped all over the world from the countries that produce it, carried in huge ships called oil tankers. If one of these massive ships runs into rocks or springs a leak in a storm, the oil escapes into the ocean. Oil floats on top of water, and huge rafts of drifting oil are deadly for all types of marine life.

A penguin caught in an oil slick would lose the insulation provided by its feathers, so it would freeze in the cold water. Oil is also toxic, and swallowing too much of it could poison the birds. And when they're covered in the sticky oil, they can't swim and find food for themselves or their young. Oil spills from tankers have killed millions of penguins.

Warming Water, Melting Ice

There's another problem for penguins that we humans have created: climate change. Human-caused air pollution makes our planet's temperature rise, and the effects of the climate shift are being felt all over the world. And this warming trend hits the penguins' habitats especially hard.

Global warming is having a terrible effect on the icy world of the Antarctic penguins. In other areas, the exact temperature doesn't make such a big difference. If the temperature in a desert, prairie, or forest warms by two degrees, not much changes, at least not right away. But if the temperature of ice and snow rises, every-thing changes fast. Ice begins to melt at 32°F. Even a tiny rise above 32°F triggers melting.

Emperor penguins raise their young directly on the sea ice. With their short legs, they can't easily clamber around on steep, rocky land. And they can't fly to a new breeding ground. They need the flat expanses of sea ice where they can move around and get in and out of the water without difficulty. Without sea ice, Emperors won't have a place to breed. Or if cracks appear in the melting ice before their chicks have had a chance to grow warm, waterproof feathers, they may fall into the sea and die.

Adult penguins are usually fine with being in cold water. But during one month of the year, they have to stay dry. This is the time when they molt, which means they shed their feathers to make room for new ones. They do this before the cold season begins so they can start the winter with a fresh warm coat. While the birds are molting, they need firm sea ice to stand on. But as temperatures are now getting warmer, that sea ice is vanishing.

The second largest rookery of Emperor penguins used to be at a place called Halley Bay in Antarctica. Every year, about twenty thousand breeding pairs of penguins would flock there to raise their young. But starting in 2016 almost no penguin babies survived—not just one year, but three years in a row—due to early melting of sea ice. The rookery has all but disappeared, although some of the penguins may have moved to another place nearby to try again.

The penguins' world is changing.

There are now approximately five hundred thousand Emperor penguins, but scientists fear that two-thirds of them could disappear by 2050 if sea ice continues to melt as fast as it's melting today.

Another big problem for penguins is a lack of food. Hotter temperatures also make it harder for fish and other ocean life to survive. Krill in particular need the water to remain cold. The population of this crustacean in the warming southern oceans has gone down tremendously, by as much as 80 percent since the 1970s. Without those krill, penguins have much less to eat.

Where Are All the Fish?

Fish are a really important food source for penguins, and they're also great food for people. Fish are not only delicious—they're also nourishing, filled with protein, vitamins, and nutrients. Hungry humans all over the world eat fish. But there isn't an unlimited number of them in the sea.

Penguins are competing with humans for food. And in that competition, humans are winning. Huge fishing ships are like enormous floating factories, with giant nets that scoop up millions of fish. When so many fish are taken, there aren't enough fish left to lay eggs, so the number of fish starts going down. This is called overfishing. Almost all species of fish in a penguin's home waters are badly overfished.

African and Humboldt penguins are especially affected by overfishing. They depend on two kinds of small fish: sardines and anchovies. These fish are favorites of people as well, and too many of them are being taken from the sea. Whole colonies of penguins have died from starvation as fish populations drop lower and lower.

Penguins are also at risk from getting tangled in fishing gear made of super-strong plastic cords and nets. Penguins sometimes get scooped up when big fishing vessels drag giant nets through the ocean as they try to catch as many fish as possible. Also, if fishing nets and lines break loose from the ship, they can float for years. These drifting masses of lines, nets, and hooks are called ghost gear. A penguin that gets too close to ghost gear can get tangled up. If the penguin can't free itself, it will drown.

Fighting Back

For a long time, scientists weren't too worried about many penguin species, as their numbers seemed to be holding steady. But as fewer and fewer fish are left in the oceans and climate change heats up the planet, penguin populations are getting smaller at record rates.

Fortunately, many wildlife researchers are keeping careful watch over all the different species of penguins and their habitats. Scientists from the Global Penguin Society, Penguins International, and other organizations track penguins at sea and monitor penguin colonies on land, counting how many there are and how many chicks they have. As we get more information, it's clear some species of penguins are more at risk than we thought.

Many penguin researchers feel that penguins should be given more protection. Right now, for example, Emperor penguins are only listed on the IUCN Red List as Near Threatened, but many people are urging that they be reclassified and given the more serious status of Endangered. And other penguin species may soon join the Emperors on the endangered species list.

So what does the future hold for these

Penguins need our support.

beautiful black-and-white birds? How can they overcome so many complicated problems? People all over the world who love penguins are fighting to find ways to help them.

4

HELPING HANDS

Helping penguins is a challenge, because every species of penguin has unique problems and needs. But one thing all penguins depend on is a habitat where they can find food and raise their young. To save the penguins, we need to think about two habitats: the land and the ocean.

Build a House for Penguins

One of the best ways people are helping penguins is by making sure their nesting sites are

Wildlife scientists keep a careful eye on penguins.

usable. As we've seen, Humboldt penguins are threatened because there's too much guano mining in their nesting colonies, leaving the birds no place to dig their burrows. Penguins International is working with Peruvian researchers from the Punta San Juan Program to solve the problem. The researchers keep close track of nesting birds, counting every egg and studying exactly how the nests are built. Since they can't always prevent people from taking the guano, the next best option is to create shelters where the penguins can lay their eggs. That means trying to figure out which type of nest shelter would work best.

You might have put up a birdhouse in your backyard or school grounds to serve as a home for wrens or chickadees. You would probably have put it high up off the ground, and that makes sense for those types of birds. But of course, since penguins can't fly, their homes have to be right on the ground. Researchers are making shelters from concrete, plastic, or ceramic with arched roofs so the parents and babies can cuddle up snugly underneath. They can avoid wind and rain and cool off in the shade on sunny days. The secure roof helps keep away predators such as gulls that would love a snack of penguin eggs.

SOS—Save Our Seas

There's a way that the millions of penguin fans—including you!—can help penguins without traveling to the faraway places where they live. We need to get plastic out of the oceans where penguins swim, and litter starts where we live. Schools and youth groups all over the world are coming together to fight against plastic litter.

It's especially important to keep penguin nesting sites clear of plastic and other garbage. The Global Penguin Society and other organizations work with hundreds of kids and community members in South America and countries around the world to remove trash from areas used by penguins. And every piece of litter picked up is one that won't drift to the oceans and possibly end up in a penguin's stomach.

In the United States, there are thousands of miles of beaches where plastic trash washes up. Kids living in Nome, Alaska, picked up trash from beaches on the Bering Sea. Students from Seabreeze Elementary School in Jacksonville, Florida, picked up litter on Atlantic Ocean beaches. They had an extra-big job after a hurricane had trashed the beach, blowing in even more plastic debris than usual. The ocean-loving students were members of a club they started to protect the beaches, called the Kelp Club (kelp is a kind of seaweed).

Hundreds of students from nine Orange

Every litter pickup helps wildlife around the world.

County elementary schools in California visited Huntington Beach to pick up litter washed up by the Pacific Ocean. Some schools and youth groups on the Pacific Coast plan special cleanups on a special day called Kids Ocean Day. This tradition was started in 1994 by environmentalist Michael Klubock, a sailor who was deeply saddened by the tons of plastic trash he saw floating in the middle of the ocean.

Don't live near the beach? You can still help penguins. Sadly, plastic litter is everywhere. A piece of plastic lying on the ground can be washed away by the rain or blown by the wind till it ends up in a stream or river. And all rivers run into the sea. So picking up plastic anywhere can help penguins everywhere.

Deadly Oil

In 2000 the crew of a cargo ship called *Treasure* knew the old vessel was doomed. The ship was battered and had long needed repairs, and now a storm had broken open a hole in the side. It was only a matter of time before the ship would sink in the cold waters just off the coast of South Africa.

The crew was not in danger—they had radioed for help and would soon be airlifted to safety. But the ship held thirteen hundred gallons of fuel oil. As the ship broke up in the waves, the black, thick oil cascaded into the sea. Oil floats on top of water, and the oil spill created a huge raft of dense, sticky oil. The wind was blowing toward the coast of Africa, only six miles away, sending the oil directly toward two of the largest breeding colonies of endangered African penguins. The oil washed up on the shore just at the height of the nesting season, when the beaches were crowded with penguins and their chicks.

Immediately, conservation groups such as the Southern African Foundation for the Conservation of Coastal Birds (SANCCOB) gathered to try to help the oil-covered birds. Vets from zoos and aquariums rushed to the scene, and organizations like the International Fund for Animal Welfare and International Bird Rescue sent helpers. But even then, there were only a few hundred people available. Each bird would need hours of cleaning to scrub off the deadly oil, as well as feeding and care—and there were twenty thousand oiled birds!

A call went out for volunteers. People from all over the world came together to help save the penguins. More than twelve thousand volunteers, most of them with no wildlife experience, hurried to South Africa to help.

How do you help an oiled penguin? First, cooking oil is rubbed on the bird's feathers to soften the crust of thick fuel oil. Then the oil is washed off with a mild soap, kind of like dish detergent. Rinse and repeat. Each bird had to be washed several times to get off all the sticky oil. It took two or three volunteers to gently hold each penguin and wash it. Then

Bird with volunteer.

the volunteers would release the penguin into a pool of clean water, where it could swim around for a final rinse.

Each hungry penguin had to be hand-fed frozen fish. And the fuzzy penguin chicks, separated from their parents during the cleaning process, missed their usual warm snuggles with their parents. Part of the volunteers' job was to cuddle the frightened babies.

Meanwhile, thousands of penguins had not yet been harmed by the oil spill, but fuel oil was still clogging the beaches and seawater. More volunteers gently herded twenty thousand healthy penguins into large boxes. The captured penguins were trucked hundreds of miles away and then released. By the time they swam home days later, the oil had washed away and the sea was clear again.

Sadly, two thousand of the penguins were too badly oiled to survive. But after weeks of backbreaking, round-the-clock work, the rescuers had saved 90 percent of the birds. The methods of cleaning and feeding they invented during the crisis have helped save many more oiled birds. Oil spills continue to threaten many species of penguins every year.

An Old Lady in the Zoo

Penguins are some of the most popular animals in zoos everywhere. Crowds of people gather to watch them waddle and cuddle with each other, or leap into their saltwater pool and zoom through the water. Curious penguins will often swim right up to the glass wall of their aquarium, so close that penguin watchers are almost nose-to-nose with their favorite birds.

Penguins are difficult animals to keep in zoos, though. If you've ever tried to keep fish in a tank, you know how hard it is to keep the water clean and clear. Penguin pools take constant maintenance. And penguins need plenty of room to swim. They need a really big tank with thousands of gallons of water carefully filtered to keep it free of germs.

The birds also need places on land to enjoy sunshine and hang out with their mates. Zookeepers have to watch the temperature closely, as penguins can easily overheat. They can also get fungus infections and diseases. And you can't have just one penguin in the zoo— the sociable birds need lots of other penguins around.

In the wild, a penguin's lifespan is likely to be about fifteen to twenty-five years, but in a well-run zoo they can live much longer. A female African penguin named ET celebrated her forty-third birthday in the Metro Richmond Zoo in Virginia. The little penguin was named in 1982, the year the famous movie *E.T. the Extra-Terrestrial* came out. On her birthday, the zoo staff made her a special cake of ice and frozen fish.

ET was cuddly and friendly with humans, and she was a favorite of the zoo staff, especially Jessica Gring, who helps care for the zoo's forty-two penguins. ET and her mate, Einstein, a thirteen-year-old male, had a private pool with a special step so she could climb in and out of the water. "She and Einstein get along fantastically, even though she's older than he is," said Jessica. ET had outlived two other mates.

Because they are used to warmer temperatures than many other species of penguins, African penguins are easier to keep in captivity. About nine hundred African penguins live in US zoos. And one of the best things about zoos is that endangered species of animals can have babies in a safe environment, which helps to increase the population.

"African penguins have been listed as endangered since 2010 and have decreased in population by ninety-five percent over the last hundred years," says Jim Andelin, the zoo's director. "Fortunately, with our breeding program here, we've had some good luck with them." The Metro Richmond Zoo has had almost three hundred penguin chicks hatch since 1995. ET was mother to a dozen chicks of her own before becoming a grandmother.

Seeing penguins up close in zoos is a way

Only an inch of aquarium glass separates zoo penguins from their fans.

for people to get to know penguins—and once you get to know a penguin, it's pretty hard not to fall in love.

Adopting Nino, DJ, and Sir Wil O. Pingo 1st

Six-year-old Wyatt Herschell got hooked on penguins when he took a trip to a zoo in

Pittsburgh. "I saw the penguins and I was up against the glass for an hour," Wyatt said. For his next birthday, he asked guests to bring donations for penguins instead of gifts.

Wyatt has a lot of stuffed penguin toys, but he's decided to adopt some real penguins. He doesn't get to keep them in his bedroom, though—Nino and DJ, two penguins he named and adopted from the Aquarium of Niagara in New York, still live with their friends and family in their tank at the aquarium. Many zoos and conservation organizations have a virtual adoption program where you can contribute money to help penguins and then receive photographs and information about "your" penguin. The money donated goes to help take care of zoo penguins and fund penguin research and rescues.

Over the years, Wyatt has planned fundraisers and raised more than seven thousand dollars to adopt penguins in zoos around the country. In 2022, on Valentine's Day, he adopted his fourteenth penguin to show his love for penguins. Of Nino and DJ, he says, "I guess I just love their cuteness and the way they waddle."

Kids all over the world are doing the same thing. A group of students from South Africa's Stellenbosch Thuthuka school raised money to adopt twelve penguins through the wildlife organization SANCCOB. The money they raised goes to help SANCCOB's work with endangered penguins, including care for orphaned chicks and oiled or injured penguins. As part of the program, students get to name their penguins. The Thuthuka students chose some creative names, including Frodo, Snafu,

Roelfie, Finrek, and Sir Wil O. Pingo 1st. The students even got to visit SANCCOB and meet some penguins in person.

Penguins in the Future

When people come together, they can do a lot to help wildlife, including penguins. Governments of nations need to work together too. The Antarctic, where millions of penguins live, doesn't belong to any one country. In 1959 many nations signed a treaty making an agreement to protect Antarctica and all its resources, including wildlife. We need more nations to pass laws protecting other parts of animal habitats. For example, Robben Island, the site of the *Treasure* oil spill and still an important nesting site for penguins, was made a protected nature preserve by South Africa in 2019.

The world would be a sadder place without penguins tobogganing across the snow, waddling on the beaches, and hanging out on the icebergs. And the cold southern seas would seem barren without the black-and-white birds winging through the water. But as long as people all around the globe are working to save penguins, we can keep the birds in the feathery tuxedos thriving in their cold, wet world.

Together we can save the penguins.

FUN FACTS ABOUT THE BIRDS THAT WEAR TUXEDOS

1. How do you tell male and female penguins apart? It isn't easy! Male and female penguins look almost exactly alike. Males are usually slightly larger, with longer beaks.

2. Penguins do a lot of singing, especially when it's mating time, but their song isn't necessarily musical like some birds' songs are—penguin singing is often compared to the braying of a donkey.

3. Each penguin gives a special call that its

family can recognize. Emperor penguins recognize each other's voices even if they haven't seen each other for months.

4. Penguin eyeballs work best underwater. On land, they don't see as clearly. That may be one reason why they will sometimes walk right up to humans.

5. Besides penguins, there are about forty species of birds that can't fly. Other non-flyers include emus, kiwis, and ostriches.

6. Like all birds, penguins don't have teeth. Sharp spines on the roofs of their beaks help them grab and hold slippery, wriggling fish.

7. Many kinds of penguins will eat small sharp rocks, which help them grind up food inside their digestive systems.

8. A penguin's short legs only let it walk at about two miles an hour. Most humans walk at about three miles an hour or faster. Penguins aren't great at climbing uneven surfaces and do best on flat land or ice. However, Rockhopper penguins are good at—you guessed it—hopping on rocks.

9. Emperor penguins incubate their eggs for longer than any other bird in the world. Emperor dads keep their eggs warm for more than two months.

10. Where do penguins get a drink if all the fresh water is frozen into ice? Unlike most creatures, penguins can drink seawater because they have a special gland inside their bodies that filters the extra salt out of their blood.

11. Penguins often have trouble keeping cool. In South America, where Humboldt penguins live, the temperature can reach the nineties (Fahrenheit) or hotter! These penguins have bare pink patches with no feathers on their heads that help them give off extra body heat.

HOW YOU CAN HELP SAVE THE PENGUINS

Even though they live so far away from most of us, penguins are counting on us! There's a lot we can do to help these feathered friends.

1. Have a penguin party! World Penguin Day is on April 25, and that's a good time to celebrate these beautiful birds. Consider working with an adult to use social media to spread the word about penguins and their problems.

2. Remember that World Ocean Day falls on June 8 each year. On that day, Penguins

International encourages people to #PickUp4Penguins. Pick up thirty pieces of trash to help meet the goal of protecting 30 percent of our planet by 2030.

3. Organize a stream bank or beach cleanup. It's especially important to penguins that we keep our beaches free of plastic litter. Not just ocean beaches—any stream, creek, or river eventually runs into the sea. Visit this site for some tips from the National Environmental Education Foundation: NeefUSA.org/nature/land/tips-organizing-beach-clean.

4. Use the power of art to spread the word about penguins and the reasons so many of them are endangered. Draw, paint, photograph, write, dance, and sing—use your imagination to attract attention to

penguins and how amazing they are.

5. Dream up creative ways to raise money for penguin research, nest boxes, or oil-spill rescues. You can set up bake sales, raffles, or art sales. What else can you think of? Here are some organizations that can use donations to help penguins:

- Penguins International. They put up nest boxes for Humboldt penguin families and support Emperor and Gentoo penguin research. You can find out more at PenguinsInternational.org.

- The Global Penguin Society. They have protected forty-two million acres of penguin habitat. Find out more at GlobalPenguinSociety.org.

- SANCCOB. They raise orphaned

penguin chicks and help clean
and care for birds after oil spills.
See SANCCOB.co.za.

6. Adopt an Emperor penguin chick. You
   don't have to hold him on your feet, fortunately. You or your class could sym-
   bolically adopt an Emperor or many
   other species of penguins. The adoption
   fee goes to help wildlife conservation
   efforts. Here are a couple of organizations that offer penguin adoptions:

   • World Wildlife Fund:
     Gifts.WorldWildlife.org/gift-center

   • Oceana: Gift.Oceana.org
     /collections/adopt-a-penguin

7. Check out March of the Penguin Mad-
   ness in the spring. Vote for your favorite
   zoo penguin in March every year. The

winning penguin gets an (imaginary) ice crown—and a lot of helpful publicity for penguin research. Find out more about the event at PenguinsInternational.org /march-of-the-penguin-madness.

8. Brainstorm ways you can use less oil in your daily life. Oil spills harm thousands of penguins every year. The less oil we use, the less that has to be carried in ships that travel through penguin habitats. Remember, it's not just fuel for cars—many power plants that produce electricity are run on oil. Also, plastic is made from petroleum oil.

9. Make your home or your school more eco-friendly. The National Wildlife Federation's Eco-Schools USA program helps students learn many ways to

"green" your backyard and schoolyard, as well as home and school buildings, including using less oil, reducing electricity use, recycling, and creating less litter. Every person living in a more environmentally friendly way helps penguins and lots of other wildlife too.

10. Are there penguins in your future? Research ways to pursue a career helping wildlife. If working to protect wildlife is your hobby, maybe it could become your job! Here are some places to start:

- The Wildlife Society: Wildlife.org /wildlife-careers
- LiveAbout: LiveAbout.com/careers -with-wildlife-125918
- National Wildlife Federation: NWF.org

11. Write to your representatives in state

and local government. Make it clear you want them to take strong action on protecting endangered species. (Their contact info is available on the internet.) For instance, even though penguins don't live in the United States, putting species of penguins on the US endangered species list helps them. A good example is that US fishing vessels have to take extra care not to harm penguins because they are on the list.

12. VOTE! It helps endangered species whenever we vote for political candidates who support environmental protection. Register to vote as soon as you're old enough, and encourage your family to vote with saving the environment (and penguins!) in mind.

REFERENCES

Borboroglu, Pablo García, and P. Dee Boersma, editors. *Penguins: Natural History and Conservation.* Seattle: University of Washington Press, 2013.

DeNapoli, Dyan. *The Great Penguin Rescue: 40,000 Penguins, a Devastating Oil Spill, and the Inspiring Story of the World's Largest Animal Rescue.* New York: Free Press, 2010.

Free, Cathy. "A Penguin Love Story: At 43, She's the World's Oldest African Penguin. Her Mate Is 13." *The Washington Post*, February 14, 2023. washingtonpost.com/lifestyle/2023/02/14/worlds-oldest-african-penguin-zoo.

Global Penguin Society. "Learn About Penguins."

Info & News. Accessed July 31, 2023.
globalpenguinsociety.org/#species.

Green, Kayla. "12-Year-Old Adopts Pair of Penguins
from Aquarium of Niagara, Has Raised $7K for
Penguin Conservation." *News 4*, WIVB, February
18, 2022. wivb.com/news/12-year-old-adopts
-pair-of-penguins-from-aquarium-of-niagara-has
-raised-7k-for-penguin-conservation.

National Geographic for Kids. "Emperor Penguin."
Animals: Birds. Accessed July 31, 2023. kids
.nationalgeographic.com/animals/birds/facts
/emperor-penguin.

Penguins International. "About Us and How We Are
Making a Difference." Accessed July 31, 2023.
penguinsinternational.org/about-us.

Southern African Foundation for the Conservation of
Coastal Birds (SANCCOB). "Climate Change."
Projects. Accessed July 31, 2023. sanccob.co.za
/projects/climate-change.

ANITA SANCHEZ is especially fascinated by plants and animals that no one loves and by the unusual, often ignored wild places of the world. Her award-winning books sing the praises of the unappreciated: dandelions, poison ivy, tarantulas, mud puddles. Her goal is to make young readers excited about science and nature. Many years of fieldwork and teaching outdoor classes have given her firsthand experience in introducing students to the wonders of the natural world.

Photo by George Steele

You can visit Anita Sanchez online at
AnitaSanchez.com
and follow her on Twitter
@ASanchezAuthor

CHELSEA CLINTON is the author of the #1 *New York Times* bestseller *She Persisted: 13 American Women Who Changed the World*; *She Persisted Around the World: 13 Women Who Changed History*; *She Persisted in Sports: American Olympians Who Changed the Game*; *She Persisted in Science: Brilliant Women Who Made a Difference*; *Don't Let Them Disappear: 12 Endangered Species Across the Globe*; *Welcome to the Big Kids Club*; *It's Your World: Get Informed, Get Inspired & Get Going!*; *Start Now!: You Can Make a Difference*; with Hillary Clinton, *Grandma's Gardens* and *The Book of Gutsy Women: Favorite Stories of Courage and Resilience*; and, with Devi Sridhar, *Governing Global Health: Who Runs the World and Why?* She is also the Vice Chair of the Clinton Foundation, where she works on many initiatives, including those that help empower the next generation of leaders. She lives in New York City with her husband, Marc, and their children.

Photo courtesy of the author

You can follow Chelsea Clinton on Twitter
@ChelseaClinton
or on Facebook at
Facebook.com/ChelseaClinton

DON'T MISS MORE BOOKS IN THE

save the . . .
BLUE WHALES
Christine Taylor-Butler
With an introduction by Chelsea Clinton

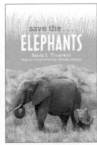

save the . . .
ELEPHANTS
Sarah L. Thomson
With an introduction by Chelsea Clinton

save the . . .
FROGS
Sarah L. Thomson
With an introduction by Chelsea Clinton

save the . . .
GIRAFFES
Anita Sanchez
With an introduction by Chelsea Clinton

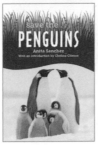

save the . . .
PENGUINS
Anita Sanchez
With an introduction by Chelsea Clinton

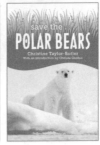

save the . . .
POLAR BEARS
Christine Taylor-Butler
With an introduction by Chelsea Clinton

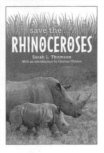

save the . . .
RHINOCEROSES
Sarah L. Thomson
With an introduction by Chelsea Clinton

save the... SERIES!

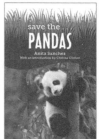

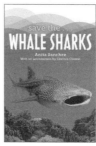